# Church Chuckles

Thursday night: potluck dinner. Prayer and medication to follow.

Written by

Ellen P. Blooming
Paul Seaburn

new seasons™

*E*mily was having a little
difficulty with the Lord's
prayer: "Our father, who does
art in heaven…"

As several church ladies got up to prepare for a buffet, our minister announced, "The ladies leaving the sanctuary will have some hot buns for us after the service."

$O$ur pastor will be
attending a weekend seminar
on mental illnesses. Please pray
for his sane return.

# CHURCH NOTES

*U*shers will eat latecomers.

# SERVICE NOTICE

*I*f all of the pews are full when you arrive, please wait in the aisle for help from one of the pushers.

A church can never have
enough dogma—bring pets this
Sunday for the blessings of
the animals service.

You could tell Father Jim was happy with his sermon because he ended by saying, "Many have yawned, but few are dozin'."

*P*art-time secretary needed to answer church phone and give massages to the Pastor.

*R*everend Ryan was definitely on a diet when he said, "Be good, low-carb Christians and do not partake of the forbidden fruits."

*T*hursday night: potluck dinner. Prayer and medication to follow.

## SERVING OPPORTUNITIES

The pastor would appreciate it if the ladies of the congregation would lend him their electric girdles for the pancake breakfast next Sunday.

# CHURCH NOTES

*L*atecomers are asked to wait until the service is over to be seated.

Amanda explained why
she brought her dolls to
Sunday school: "I'm building
a Tower of Barbie."

*F*orgive me, Father, for I have sinned. I snuck in with my two kids in the trunk.

*L*adies, don't forget the rummage sale. It's a good chance to get rid of those things not worth keeping around the house. Bring your husbands.

*E*very year around April 15,
our pastor likes to give a
sermon warning us to beware
of false profits.

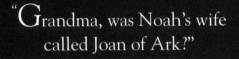

"Grandma, was Noah's wife
called Joan of Ark?"

*T*onight's sermon topic:
"What is Hell?"
Come early and listen to
our choir practice.

# CHURCH NOTICE

The peacekeeping meeting scheduled for today has been canceled due to a conflict.

# FAMILY NEWS

Single mother workshops have been canceled until father notice.

Our pastor is a real comedian. He calls the Ten Commandments: "God's Top Ten Signs You May Not Be Going to Heaven."

"My pastor says you
must love your neighbor,
even if you hate him."

*D*eacon Steve is our Internet preacher. His sermons are always filled with references to e-mail, e-commerce, and e-pistles.

*I*f you're a carpenter, or
searching for The Carpenter,
our town has what you're
looking for.

*L*ittle Wayne could always be found sitting under the Christmas tree singing his favorite song: "A Wayne in the Manger."

John and Susan have been lifelong friends. This marriage marks the end of that friendship.

Make singing a habit.

Mark explained to his parents, "Jesus used to fly on an airplane, and Pontius was the pilot!"

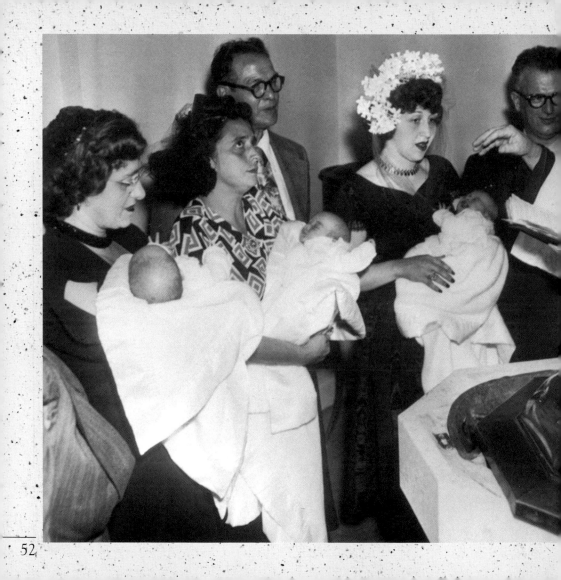

This afternoon there will be a meeting in the south and north ends of the church. Children will be baptized at both ends.

Our guest speaker is a prison minister who will talk about Christian felonship.

The bride nearly fainted when Reverend Hal asked, "Do you, Robert, take Melinda to be your awful wedded wife?"

"*L*et us bow our heads in prayer for the many who are sick of our church and community."

# FAMILY NEWS

Wednesday at 5 P.M. there will be a meeting of the Little Mothers' Club. All wishing to become Little Mothers, please see the minister in his study.

# CHURCH HAPPENINGS

The Church is saving aluminum cans, bottles, and other items to be recycled. Proceeds will be used to cripple children.

Our pastor is a fan of reality shows. He says: "I am your holy plastic surgeon, here to give you a faith lift."

Mickey told his mom he was afraid the pastor would throw an egg at him because in his sermon he said: "Take my yoke upon you."

The baptismal pool repairs have been postponed for a week because Reverend Atkins has been feeling under the water.

# SERVING OPPORTUNITIES

We also need a few more volunteers to help with monthly potlucks due to the large members attending.

# SERVICE NOTICE

*L*atecomers are asked to use the back entrance because church members are disturbed.

*D*on't let worry kill you.
The Church can help.

A little boy's prayer: "Dear God, please take care of Daddy and Mommy and my sister and my brother and me. And please take care of yourself, God. If anything happens to you, we're gonna be in a big mess."